I PRAY

Written by Rachel Windham

Illustrated by Erin Casteel

I Pray
By Rachel Windham
Copyright © 2012 by Rachel Windham

Additional copies of this book are available from the publisher:

Rachel Windham
300 E. McNeese St. Suite 3-A
Lake Charles, LA 70605
rachel_windham@suddenlink.net

Printed in the
United States of America

Dedicated to

Gabriel and Autumn Windham

Your childhood prayers inspired this book. May your communication with God increase as you grow into the young adults He created you to be.

"Now I lay me down to sleep.
I pray the Lord my soul to keep."

"Thank you, God, for this day!"

"God, I thank you for this food.
Help me to grow up big and strong."

"Jesus, please touch my boo-boo."

I pray...
...When I am sad, angry, or upset.
Sometimes I pray for my pet.

"God, bless children all around the world."

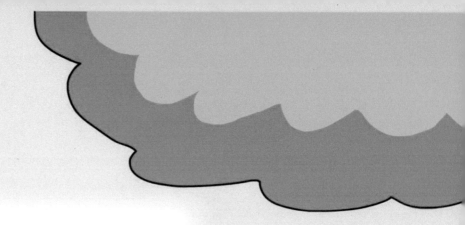

I pray...
...For others who are in need
And for those who help out
with their good deeds.

"God, please help the fireman rescue the kitty."

"God, bless the President of the United States, and bless my neighbor, Mr. Elmo, and bless the missionaries in Africa."

I pray...
...For forgiveness when I've done wrong
And that God helps me to grow up strong.

"God, please forgive me for not sharing my toys.
I want to be a nice person."

"God, thank you for sunshine and puppies."

I pray...
...For problems
...And people
...And pets
...And food

Prayer is simply talking to God.

You can talk to God about anything or anyone.

You can ask God to bless those you love.

You can ask Him to help others who are hurting.

When you do not know how to help someone, you can always pray.
God can help them and be with them even when you cannot.

Sometimes, you may tell God "Thank you" for the things that you like.
This is praying, too.

You can even talk to God about yourself.

You can tell Him EVERYTHING! He will always keep your secrets.

You can tell God your troubles and your fears. He will never laugh at
you or make fun of you.

If it's important to you, then it's important to God.

God is all around, even though you can't see Him.

When you talk to Him, He listens.

You are important to God.

My Keepsake Prayer Record

My goodnight prayer:

_____

_____

_____

Before I eat, I thank God for my food this way:

_____

_____

_____

People I have prayed for:

_____

_____

_____

_____

Places I sometimes pray:

_____

_____

_____

Prayer Activity and Bible Study

In the Bible, people sent pieces of cloth to others in hopes that their need would be met. "God did powerful things through Paul, things quite out of the ordinary. The word got around and people started taking pieces of clothing— handkerchiefs and scarves and the like—that had touched Paul's skin and then touching the sick with them. The touch did it—they were healed and whole." Acts 19:11-12 (The Message Bible)

In the same way, you can send a prayer token to someone you care about. In the back of the book is a prayer poem for you to give to someone. This will let that person know that you have prayed a special prayer for him or her.

I sent a special prayer token

To: _____

Date: _____

I prayed the following prayer:

_____

_____

_____

_____

_____

_____

_____

_____

_____

Rachel Windham is a published author who resides in Louisiana with her husband and their two teen-aged children. Her two passions are God and family. Through her devotional books, she hopes to give families tools to inspire and enrich their relationships with Jesus Christ. See what is happening in Rachel's world by visiting her website, rachelwindham.weebly.com. You may contact her at rachel_windham@suddenlink.net.

Erin Casteel is a native of Sulphur, Louisiana. She is an art teacher, illustrator, local mural painter, and "Ignorance Is Bliss" comic strip creator. Erin illustrated the book, The Adventures of *Red Feather Wild Horse of Corolla* and *Kyser the Singing Schnauzer*. She is a charter member and Art Director for the Southwest Louisiana Children's Book Writers and Illustrators Guild. In her spare time, Erin likes to juggle, read, tutor math, and participate in community art shows.

Acknowledgements

Rachel:
-God for giving me this opportunity.

-My wonderful husband, Eddie, who is my number one fan and supporter.
Thank you for always going the extra mile for me.
-Annette Jones, who envisioned including prayer cloths in my children's books.
This idea evolved into the prayer-token poem.
-Kelly Leake, whose friendship, prayer, and encouragement have been a part of every phase of this project.
-Pam Eddings and Sherri Price -editors extraordinaire.

Thanks to each of you. You took the "im" out of impossible to make this work a reality. I'm blessed by all you contribute.

Erin:
-Mom, for being my biggest encouragement, critic, and fan.
-Dad, for sharing my sense of humor and making every day an adventure.
-Michael, for being impressed with the things I do.
-Courtney, for being a fan and fellow artist.

I pray
When I go to bed at night
And the sun is out of sight
I pray
As I'm sitting very still
At the table before each meal
I pray
When a boo-boo I have found
After falling on the ground
I pray
For people who are far and near
Unknown strangers and friends so dear
I pray
For forgiveness when I've done wrong
And that God helps me to grow up strong
I pray
Any time, anywhere
Because I know God's always near
I pray for problems and people and pets and food
I pray for me
And I pray for YOU!!

I prayed for you today.

Signed,

_____

Made in the USA
Columbia, SC
07 April 2024

33912507R00024